Bonami

The Spinster's Poems
101 Bonaku

T0284595

Karma

Richard Prince

Foreword

Last Laugh.

Bloated. Mad. Deep Bleep. Link Stink.
Open close. Paint your nose. Stop sleep
bark. Pimple lie. Giant gym. Maybe better.
Tool. Me and me 2.

Sounds like bird talk. Or some psychic
jujitsu left over from an interview
with JG Ballard. Some of these word
jobs would make good descriptions for
Katz&Dogg weed strains. (Cowboy Plenty)

"Boring snoring simply boring no need
of snoring."

Could be an improv comment under an
Instagram portrait.

But it's not. Not yet. Not ever.

I'm just punching the lines of Bonami's
Spinster's Poems.

Punching the punchline.

Morse Code. Clouds full of acorns. Waves
of survival. The trial is about to begin.
When there's "barking" at the door? There's
101 bonaku reasons not to let the dog in.

Voices and drums are two of them.

The poems are a shoe in. Your fantasy
becomes swollen. And if she looks like
you? You're "on your own." Like he says

in "Lots"—you are not matter. And if you
are? You're probably dead in the water.

The poems are elastic bands of sound
that are out loud on pages of paper
settled in black ink that touch us
with loneliness, missing memory, nice
good scale, painted noses, card board
coffins, and crowded farts.

Nice scale.

Again.

Nice scale.

I said it again because good scale is
enough. Don't believe me. Believe him.
Everything is wrong if it's not nice.
And if it's not nice it's not good.

The door. The building. The street. The
country. The whole "not enough" planet
is not enough. It's all about secret
handshakes and the cosmic groove.

Can you goofy the groove under the tube?
Or do you soak it. Wash. Rinse. Dry.

Is your skin in the game?

Try screaming next to a fallen tree.
(Maybe you won't hear the tree but at
least you'll hear yourself.) Then? Then
wait for the beep. And if you don't
escape the rebel yell, don't get mad
and blame me. It's not my revolution.

I'm only interested in what lasts.
Believe me, the towel that you throw in
will leave you wet and naked, and under
the thumb of "others in tears."

Smash and grab that second opinion.
Interpretation fades and forgets.
You're the one who opens. (Not closes.)
Speculation, judgment, opinion.
Subjectivity. They all rot and worm
the heart. If love is not awake then
sleeping is all you need.

Giving up and giving in are not the
same. (We would rather be up than in.)
That's the option. "Avoid." As long
as you're alive avoid death. That's
the "best" I can come up with. Sounds
simple. Sure. But then I always steal
to avoid.

Remember.

Stop before it's too late. Or go before
it's too early. As long as your love is
"bouncing" and half choking, your bloody
pink mood will frap and "itch" and turn
blue, and in the end, "close the deal."

Continue.

Contribute.

Autograph the dotted line.
(A I your initials.)

Bonami isn't some ancient mahogany heirloom. (Solid. Dependable. Reliable.) He's more shapeshifting, mercurial, wayward. He calls to mind a Fairport Convention. A mainstay that's always maintaining new pastures. No muddy footprints. No commanding membership. No slog or tramp. No reaching for stars in the time of your life.

This time he's more Elizabethan troubadour immersed in a pastoral melodicism. A purposeful formative steamer with an earthy rhythmic crunch. Topsy-turvy celebrations on the musing transience of his own epitaph.

"Like it or not, the same is..."

If you don't want to stink don't get in the elevator. Take the stairs. The building will eventually end somewhere north of the 13th floor. When you roof you'll be able to smell the shit falling from the green-screen sky.

Jigs and jams. Zigs and zags. If you survive the hangman's noose three times, they let you go.

No questions asked.

Question: "Gottle O'Geer" was a 1976 funk instrumental by which group...?
Traffic
The Neon Boys

Blind Faith
Sir Douglas Quintet
None of the above.

Solid turf.

"Si Tu Dois Partir" was written by Bob
Dylan. (There's always a segue.)

This is a margin not a principle. Chains
of reason are tossed, erased when you're
on the edge, in the scrum, eating the
fringe, the verge, the hem.

Trademark. We've all got our schticks.
Adopted personas, signatures, and stock
replies.

Hamburger costumes and last laughs.

After forty years, my costume is still
nailed to the chicken crossing the
street.

Why?

Satisfaction, triumph, success. But then
there are consequences. Being scorned
or regarded as a failure. (So what else
is new?) Next time you're bullied or
heckled, repeat back what you heard.
"A laugh a laugh before you realize will
be the last."

If you happen to be the last person
laughing the last laugh laughs best.
You're not alone. There's always a gang
plank. Sample it.

The worst thing that can happen is
you'll fall off onto an island and turn
into a triangle and a message.

Make sure when your ship comes in you're
not at the airport.

Right now I can hear you knocking,
outside, fueling the flags of riot.

I don't think wishful. And I never
hope not.

In the end there's not much at stake.

Truth be told.

I'll tell.

I'll tell you everything.

I think this world is another planet's
hell.

splattered on the wall
fame as a fart
inside an elevator
crowded
like it
or not
the same
is

Whining dissent
the square emptying
out
while his bloated face
smile
the others in
tears

what is
the best
option
for you
if not
avoid
death
as long
as you are
alive

Mad

Mad as mad
You
Can
Mad
As mad
You want
Just Mad
As Mad
You
Not
me
please

shit balls
falling
from the sky
truth bouncing
from the side
you lie
from inside
love stretched
but is
mine

Dream
like
scream
sleep
deep deep
waiting
for the beep
I look out
And
Weep

Monday
Like
Sunday
Stinks
You
Download
Any
Link
While
Your
Mother
blink
while
the
lover
put
on
her
finger
a
chainlink

NOT sure
At All
Never sure
Always
But
Always
Happy
To
Know
That
Sure
Is NOT
Enough

In house
delirium
but
not
without
a laugh
a laugh
before
you
realize
will
be
the
last

Wrong
Key
Wrong
Door
Wrong
Building
Wrong
Street
Wrong
City
Wrong
Country
Wrong
Planet

In
front
or
behind
the
door
the
difference
is
about
who
opens
who
closes
otherwise
we
are
the
same

Dead
cold
on
marble
top
of
kitchen
table
steaming
hot

Scale
Not
Big
Not
Small
Not
Nice
Not
Nasty
Just
right

Walk
Don't
Run
Sleep
Sleep
Sleep
More
Sleep
Better
Sleep
Now

Paint
Your
Nose
Paint
It
Better
Paint
It
Again
Paint
It
Longer
Liar

Stop
When
You
Can
Stop
If
You
Want
Stop
Before
Is
Too
Late

Sleep
Sleep
Why
Not
Sleep
If
Love
Is
Not
Awake

Sing
Sign
Sob
Stop
Simple
Sign
Stay
Sorrow

When
We
Want
Watch
We
Will
Whisper
Well

Mood
Bad
Mood
When
You
Get
Far
Time
Shrinks
Inside
My
Mind
Bad
Mood
Good

Bark
At
The
Door
Danger
Nowhere
Bark
Anywhere
Danger
Downstairs

Everywhere
Scared
Nowhere
Itch
Somewhere
Fear
There
Itch
Itch
Itch
Bare
Unbearable
Atmosphere
Don't
Move
Wait
For
Me
There

Inbetween
Myself
And
Despair
Thin
Thin
Mystere
Lettuce
To
Compare
With
Nothing
But
Just
A
Bunch
Of
Pears
With
Cheese
To
Spare
When
The
Farmer
Is
Not
Aware

Color field
Color shield
Boring Neal
Time to steal
Close the deal
Lacking will

Chopped arm
Marble clam
Cardboard box
Perfect size
For a coffin boy

Scream and cry
Pimple lie
Not a bip
The baby is
Fried

Milk the whore
Lazy bore
Coffee in bed
While her baby
Is
Dead

Never
Turn
Slowly
Down
With
Him
Behind
Unless
You
Like
To
Lose
Yours
Mind

Not
Boiling
Still
And
Yet
Ready
To
Find
A
Cheap
Thrill

Giant Gym
Stunning shush
Hand in hand
Daddy
Mummy
And him
Shameless
Fall
Over the parking
Lot

Lock the eyes
The room is wide
Weep and deep
Before i
Sleep

tatatttiiitatataaaa
deaf
to music
radio
off
sad
home
to live
in

Puf Puf Puf
Puf
pufpufpuf
Never
Thought
Last
Breath
Sound
Like
This
She's
Dead
That's
it

No
Need
No
Need
To
Stay
Inside
Outside
Good
Is
Enough

A
Space
Much
Better
A
Place

Later
Later
Before
Better
Maybe
Better

Flip
Flop
Flap
Snap
And
Act
Against
The
Hidden
Rat

Ass
Hole
You
Are
Born
Forty
Years
Still
Ass
Hole
You
Are

Weight
Loss
Loss
Loss
Weight
Up
And
Loss
Again

Around

Inside
You
Can
Outside
You
Are
Not
Free
To
Change
What
You
See
Around

Take
Care
Love
Not
What
You
Care
Love
Just
What
Is
There

Jump
Fly
Crash
Splash
Squash
Is
Useless
Anywhere
Whatever
I
Care

Yell
Yellow
Mellow
Mad
Damned

Why
Blood
Ties
When
Feeling
Lies
And
Pippo
Dies

Self
Fish
Meat
Less
Means
Nothing
Until
You
Understand
Something

Must
Urban
Mast
Urbation
Mysterious
Tool
Of
Self
Preservation

Ring
Ring
The
Answer
Sting
The
Question
Was
A
Booby
Trap
To
Steal
The
Ring

Sixty
Six
Behind
You
Recycled
Wings
In
Front
Just
Little
Time
To
Sing

Families
Like
Flies
Annoying
Bunch
Of
Flying
Lumps
Of
People
Crying
When
Relatives
Die

No
Place
Where
Honestly
Would
Stay
Ideal
Sites
Fade
Into
Reality
That
Slowly
Dies

Hard
Not
Always
Soft
Often

Nowhere
In
Mind
To
Go
No Place
Really
To
Wish
Maybe
Inside
Everywhere

Within
A
Minor
Space
A
Twist
Is
A
Bliss

Stay
Dry
Wet
Can
Be
Your
Eye
And
Yet
For
What
To
Cry

Dimming
The
Feeling
Dimming
The
Temptation
To
Try
Again
The
Mistake
Of
Trying
Again

Avoid
The
Void
Of
Any
Conversation
That
Seek
To
Express
Any
Idiotic
Preoccupation

Zero
Just
zero
Only
Zero
Essentially
Zero
simply
zero
why
not

Standing
On
A
corner
waiting
at
the
corner
like
anybody
else
even
if
you
have
just
won
a
prize
the
Nobel
prize
but
still
like
anybody
else
you
stand
waiting
at
a
corner

I
Will
be
short
very
short
maybe
too
short
yet
not
enough
short

You
could
be
just
a
bitch
and
yet
you
like
to
be
an
ugly
bitch

Nothing
to
be
proud
you
just
got
like
someone
else
a
cancer

Water
lots
of
water
more
water
until
you
will
find
out
you
are
not
matter
how
much
water
dead

The
First
Person
I fell
in
love
was
me

The
first
person
I
Cheated
Was
Me

They
Lock
me
inside
a
closet
and
I
never
came
out

I
wish
my
barber
was
dead
better
than
broke

Death
could
be
the
perfect
excuse
rather
than
explain
why
whatever
change
is
needed

Like
Like
Love
starts
with
elle
even
if
has
nothing
to do
with
Love

If
you
really
listen
you
can't
have
lunch
with
anybody
who
really
talk

How
much
you
can
wait
before
you
know
whoever
was
will
not
come

The
unfuckable
can
suddenly
appear
in
front
of
your
eyes

Like
a
rental
you
inhabit
your
love
rent
control

Small
effort
to
control
your
hybrid
desire
to
fuck
drunk
the
fattest
liar

A
fantasy
swollen
like
a
pimple
in
your
mind
pops
during
the
night

Not
Just
Deaf
But
Blind
To
All
But
Her
Or
Him
Voided
Self

She
Looks
Like
You
She
Feels
Like
Me
She
Is
Lost
On
Her
Own

Itch
Sleep
Lonely
Scratch
Not
Away
Loneliness

Blank
Feeling
Of
Blank
Memory
Feeling
Blank
Not
Missing
Memory

<u>But</u>

Taste
Touching
Skin
Not
Tasting
Anything
But
Whim

Boring
Snoring
Simply
Boring
No
Need
Of
Snoring

Maybe
Calm
But
Not
Good
Just
Dead
For
Sure

Dream
With
No
Scream
Sweet
Crashed
Under
A
Beam

Suck
The
Twine
Since
You
Are
A
Swine

Pizza
Chapati
Whatever
Is
Needed
To
Be
Aggravated

Depressing
Hand
Holding
The
Bottle
Of
Still
Water
Hating
Your
Mother

Regrets
Heal
Regrets
Heal
More
Regrets
Because
You
Have
No
Regrets
At
All

When
Wrong
Don't
Write
When
Right
Don't
Ring

Soft
You
Are
Hard
You
Wish
To
See
A
Different
Egg
On
Your
Dish

Deny
What
You
Find
To
Real
To
Lie

<u>Her</u>

You
Me
For
Her
Not
You
Just
Her

Rate
Hate
Not
Too
Late
If
You
Wish
To
Avoid
The
Wrong
Mate

Sorry
Don't
Worry
I
Was
Runned
Over
By
A
Lorry

Drip
In your
Pants
Just
Wash
Your
Hands
We
Are
Not
This
Kind
Of
Friends

Dead
I
Read
I
Got
Mad
She
Did
Not
Say
A
Word
To
Dad

Live
The
Life
Die
The
Death
Bear
The
Bore
Before
You
Close
The
Store

In
Secure
You
Must
Endure
The
Bullshit
Allure
That
Will
Not
Cure
If
You
Are
Not
Sure

Mad
Or
Sad
I
Stay
In
Bed
Until
I
Am
Dead

Pain
Rain
Drain
Mine
Only
When
It
Looks
Like
A
Stain

Nail
Screw
Your
Smile
While
You
Walk
By
Is
Dirty
Like
The
Nile

Doubt

Staring
Out
And
About
Suffering
Of
Gout
With
No
Doubt
About
Death
Now

Eat
My
Sweet
Wash
My
Sheet
Street
Where
Once
A
Day
We
Meet
If
You
Or
I
Are
Not
Too
Shy

Bonami
The Spinster's Poems
101 Bonaku

Edition of 500

© 2023 Karma Books, New York

The Spinster's Poems © Bonami
Foreword © Richard Prince

Cover: Richard Prince

All rights reserved. No part
of this publication may be
reproducedin any form or by
any electronic means without
prior written permission from
the copyright holders.

ISBN 978-1-949172-97-3